My World of Science

SOFT AND HARD

Angela Royston

Heinemann Library
Chicago, Illinois

Customer Service 888-454-2279

Visit our website at www.heinemannlibrary.com

Designed by Jo Hinton-Malivoire and Tinstar Design Limited
Originated by Blenheim Colour, Ltd.
Printed and bound in China by South China Printing Company
Photo research by Maria Joannou and Sally Smith

07 06 05 04 03
10 9 8 7 6 5 4 3 2 1

Library of Congress Cataloging-in-Publication Data
Royston, Angela.
  Soft and hard / Angela Royston.
      v. cm. – (My world of science)
Includes bibliographical references and index.
Contents: Soft and hard – Which is softer? – Which is harder? –
Choosing materials – Soft materials – Clothes – Filled with air –
Hard materials – Plastic – Concrete and stone – Hard stones –
Changing from soft to hard – Changing from hard to soft.
  ISBN 1-40340-852-1 (HC), 1-40343-165-5 (Pbk)
  1. Hardness–Juvenile literature. [1. Hardness.] I. Title.
  TA418.42 .R69 2003
  620.1'123–dc21
                                2002009437

Acknowledgments
The author and publishers are grateful to the following for permission to reproduce copyright material: p. 4 Rupert Horrox; p. 5 Chris Honeywell; pp. 6, 7, 8, 9, 10, 12, 13, 14, 15, 17, 19, 21, 22, 27 Trevor Clifford; p. 11 Chris Coggins; p. 16 Julie Hamilton/Collections; p. 18 Argos; p. 20 Jerome Yeates/Science Photo Library; pp. 23, 29 Pictor International; p. 24 J. Greenberg/Trip; p. 25 Peter Gould; p. 26 Network Photographers; p. 28 PhotoDisc.

Cover photograph by Trevor Clifford.

Some words are shown in bold, **like this.** You can find out what they mean by looking in the glossary.

Contents

Soft and Hard 4

Which Is Softer? 6

Which Is Harder? 8

Choosing Materials 10

Soft Materials 12

Clothes 14

Filled with Air 16

Hard Materials 18

Plastic 20

Concrete and Stone 22

Hard Stones 24

Changing from Soft to Hard 26

Changing from Hard to Soft 28

Glossary 30

More Books to Read 31

Index 32

Soft and Hard

These teddy bears are soft. The **material** gives way under your fingers. If you **squeeze** them, your fingers will make a **dent.**

This toy train is hard. It will not change shape if you squeeze it. Hard things make a sound when you tap them.

Which Is Softer?

Some things are softer than others. The sponge cake is softer than the **modeling** clay. But the pillow is the softest thing in the picture.

This girl is testing these things to see which is the softest. She presses each one with her fingers. The softest one is the easiest one to **squeeze.**

Which Is Harder?

The wood is harder than the orange. When the boy taps the wood it makes a loud noise. But the orange does not make a noise.

All of these things are hard. The plastic plate is harder than the table mat. The metal spoon is the hardest of them all.

Choosing Materials

Some things are made of both hard and soft **materials.** The material used for the eyes of this stuffed animal is hard. But its body is made of soft material.

These chairs are made of hard wood. Wood makes the chairs strong. But each chair has a soft seat. These are more comfortable to sit on than wood.

Soft Materials

Soft things can feel gentle against your skin. This **comforter** is filled with soft **material** to make it warm and **cozy**. The pillow and mattress are soft, too.

Soft toys can feel good to cuddle.
This stuffed animal is filled with soft
material and covered with soft **fabric.**
But the plastic used for the eyes is hard.

Clothes

It is more comfortable to wear something soft than something hard and scratchy. This boy's **fleecy** shirt is soft.

This cap has a hard **brim** at the front. The brim of the cap protects the girl's face from the sun. The rest of the cap is softer.

Filled with Air

This **inflatable** castle is made of hard, strong rubber. But it is filled with air. The air makes it soft to jump and fall on.

Bicycle tires are filled with air, too. The soft tires flatten when the bicycle goes over a bump. This makes the bicycle more comfortable to ride.

Hard Materials

Floors, walls, and many pieces of furniture are made of hard **materials.** If they were not hard they would not keep their shape.

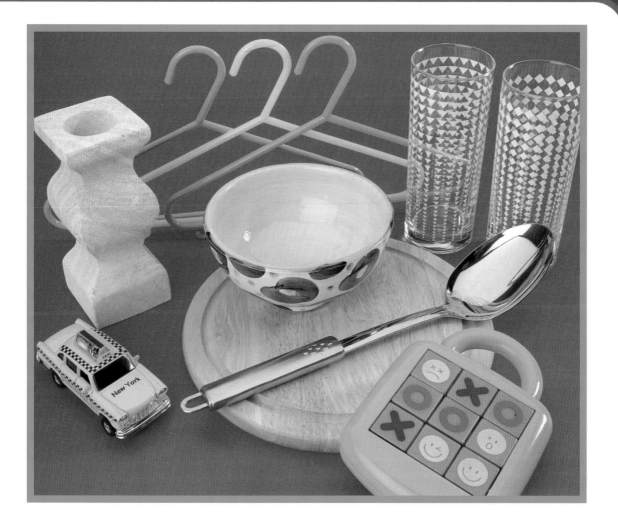

Many different materials are hard.
These things are made of stone, metal,
wood, glass, **china,** and plastic. They
each have to be hard to do their job.

Plastic

A computer is made mostly of plastic. The case is hard so that it keeps its shape. The screen is covered with hard, clear plastic.

Most kinds of plastic are hard.
Hard things often last longer
than soft things.

Concrete and Stone

This building is made of **concrete.** Concrete is made from cement, stones, and water. It becomes hard and strong when it is dry.

Stones and rocks are very hard.
Most stones and rocks have to be
dug from the ground with machines.

Hard Stones

This artist is working on a marble **statue.** Marble is a very hard stone. It is so hard that it can last for thousands of years.

Diamond is the hardest stone of all. A diamond can only be cut by another diamond.

Changing from Soft to Hard

Some things can be both soft and hard. When you put icing on a cake, the icing is soft enough to spread. A few hours later, it becomes hard!

Most things become harder when they are frozen. Peas are usually soft. They become hard when they are stored in a freezer.

hard

soft

Changing from Hard to Soft

Some things get softer when they are heated. When a candle is lit, the **wax** in the top becomes soft and melts. The wax becomes hard again when it cools.

Fruit becomes softer as it ripens. The green berries on this blackberry bush are harder than the red berries. Only the black ones are soft and ripe.

Glossary

brim flat, horizontal part of a hat or cap

china clay material used to make plates, mugs, and other things

concrete material used to make buildings and roads

cozy snug and warm

dent small dip made by pressing something

comforter soft quilt that you sleep under in bed

fabric cloth

fleecy warm, light, and fluffy

inflatable can be filled with air

material what a thing is made of

model make something into a shape

squeeze press between your hands or fingers

statue copy of a person, animal, or other shape carved out of wood, stone, or metal

wax material that gets soft when heated. Most wax comes from the ground, but some wax is made by bees

More Books to Read

Johnson, Guinevere. *Cotton*. Mankato, Minn.: The Creative Company, 1999.

Llewellyn, Claire. *Plastic*. Danbury, Conn.: Scholastic Library Publishing, 2002

Riley, Peter. *Materials*. Milwaukee: Gareth Stevens, Inc., 2002.

Index

air 16–17
clothes 14–15
concrete 22
diamond 25
fabric 13
freezing 27
icing 26
marble 24
melting 28
metal 9, 19
plastic 9, 13, 19, 20–21
ripe fruit 29
stone 19, 23, 24–25
wax 28
wood 8, 11, 19